RECYCLED DOONESBURY

SECOND THOUGHTS ON A GILDED AGE

D0691092

Doonesbury Books by G.B. Trudeau

Still a Few Bugs in the System
The President Is a Lot Smarter Than You Think
But This War Had Such Promise
Call Me When You Find America
Guilty, Guilty, Guilty!
"What Do We Have for the Witnesses, Johnnie?"
Dare to Be Great, Ms. Caucus
Wouldn't a Gremlin Have Been More Sensible?
"Speaking of Inalienable Rights, Amy . . ."
You're Never Too Old for Nuts and Berries
An Especially Tricky People
As the Kid Goes for Broke
Stalking the Perfect Tan
"Any Grooming Hints for Your Fans, Rollie?"
But the Pension Fund Was Just Sitting There
We're Not Out of the Woods Yet
A Tad Overweight, But Violet Eyes to Die For
And That's My Final Offer!
He's Never Heard of You, Either
In Search of Reagan's Brain
Ask for May, Settle for June
Unfortunately, She Was Also Wired for Sound
The Wreck of the "Rusty Nail"
You Give Great Meeting, Sid
Doonesbury: A Musical Comedy
That's Doctor Sinatra, You Little Bimbo!
Death of a Party Animal
Downtown Doonesbury
Calling Dr. Whoopee
Talkin' About My G-G-Generation
We're Eating More Beets!
Read My Lips, Make My Day, Eat Quiche and Die!
Give Those Nymphs Some Hooters!
You're Smokin' Now, Mr. Butts!

In Large Format

The Doonesbury Chronicles
Doonesbury's Greatest Hits
The People's Doonesbury
Doonesbury Dossier: The Reagan Years
Doonesbury Deluxe: Selected Glances Askance

RECYCLED DOONESBURY

SECOND THOUGHTS ON A GILDED AGE

BY G.B. TRUDEAU

Andrews and McMeel
A Universal Press Syndicate Company
Kansas City • New York

DOONESBURY is syndicated internationally by
Universal Press Syndicate.

Recycled Doonesbury: Second Thoughts on a Gilded Age
© 1990 by G.B. Trudeau. All rights reserved. Printed in
the United States of America. No part of this book may be
used or reproduced in any manner whatsoever without
written permission except in the case of reprints in the
context of reviews. For information write Andrews and
McMeel, 4900 Main Street, Kansas City, Missouri 64112.

Printed on recycled paper.

ISBN: 0-8362-1824-8
Library of Congress Catalog Number: 90-82676

"My father's talent for caricature had done him an immeasurable amount of harm professionally in New York."

— From *An Autobiography*,
by Dr. Edward L. Trudeau,
about the author's great-great
grandfather, James

PART ONE
DOG DAYS

"If we forget what we did, we won't know who we are."

— Ronald Reagan

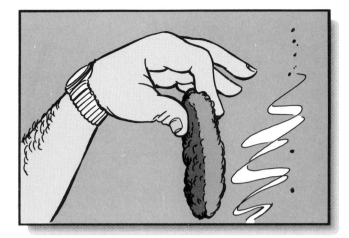

THE IMPORTANT THING, GENTLEMEN, IS **NEVER** LET IT DRY OUT! THE BURGER **MUST** REMAIN JUICY AT ALL TIMES!

THEN, GARNISH WITH IMAGINATION. AMERICANS APPRECIATE PRESENTATION!

REMEMBER, GENTLEMEN, AS GRADUATES OF THE CONTRA REHABILITATION PROGRAM, A LOT WILL BE EXPECTED OF YOU!

IF AND WHEN U.S. MILITARY SUPPORT DRIES UP THIS YEAR, YOU MUST BE ABLE TO DEMONSTRATE YOU CAN LEAVE THE FIELD AND BECOME PRO-DUCTIVE MEMBERS OF SOCIETY AGAIN!

OKAY, SAY YOUR CUSTOMER WANTS SOMETHING A BIT OUT OF THE ORDINARY, SAY A **DOUBLE** HAMBURGER. WHAT DO YOU DO? COMMANDER?

TIE HIM TO AN ANT HILL.

NO, **NO**! YOU'RE **NOT** PAYING ATTENTION!

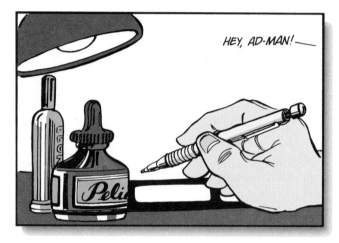

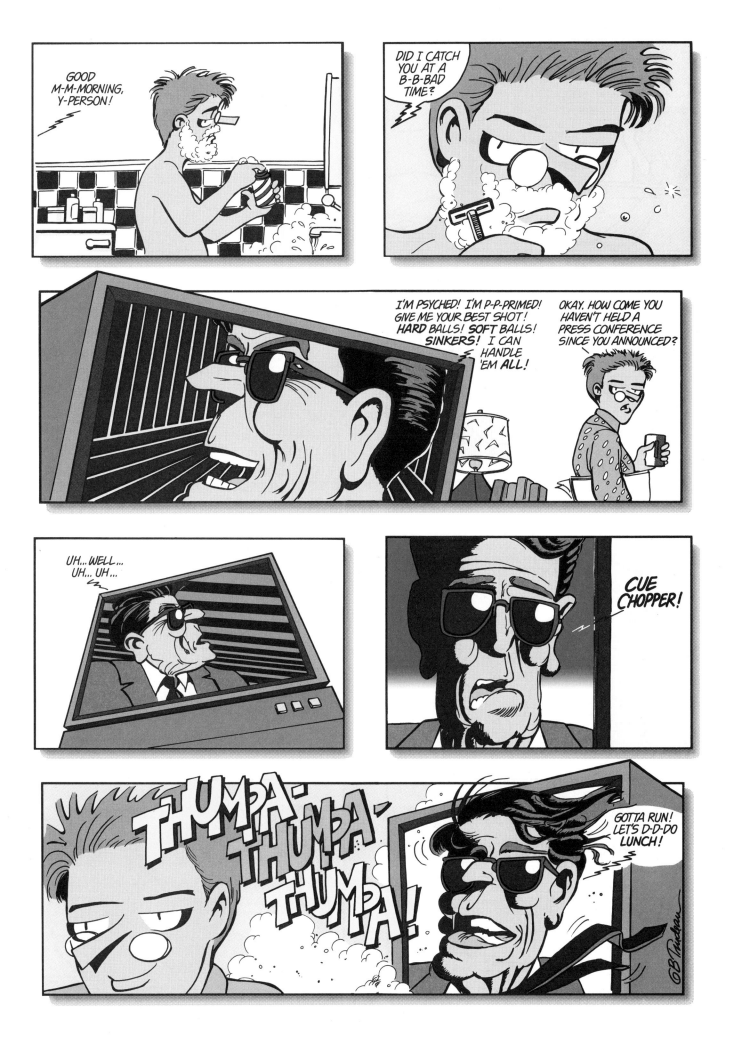

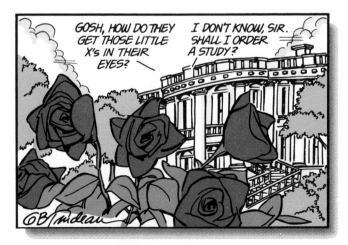

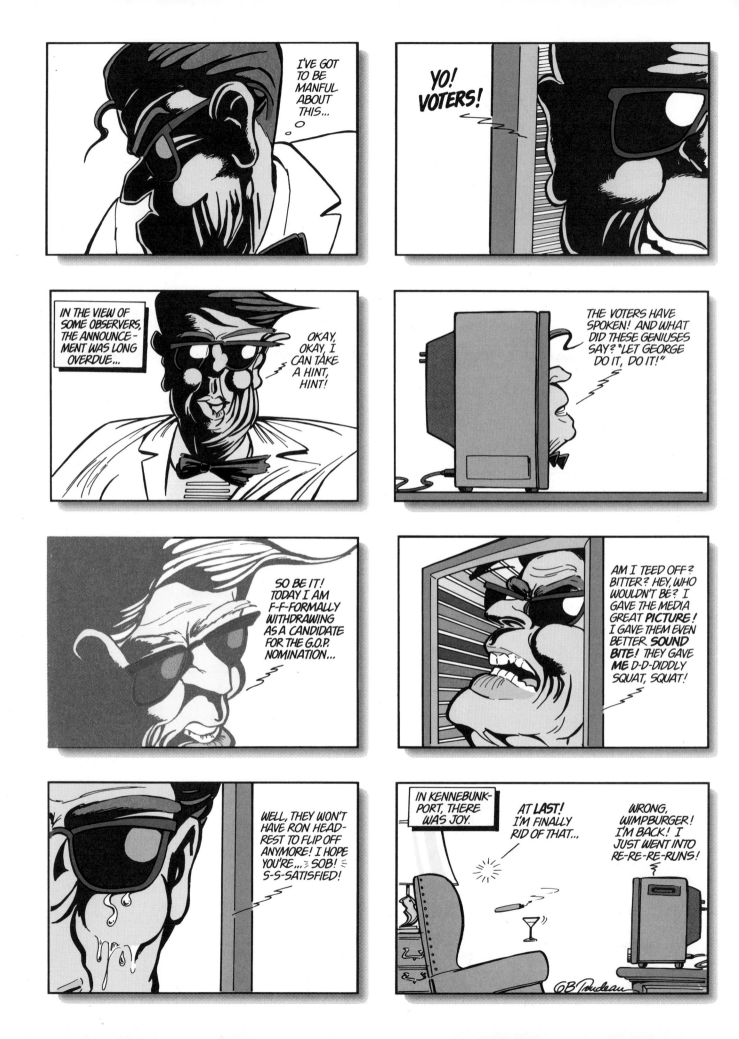

PART TWO
WHOPPERS

"If this country ever loses its interest in fishing, then we've got real trouble."
— George Bush

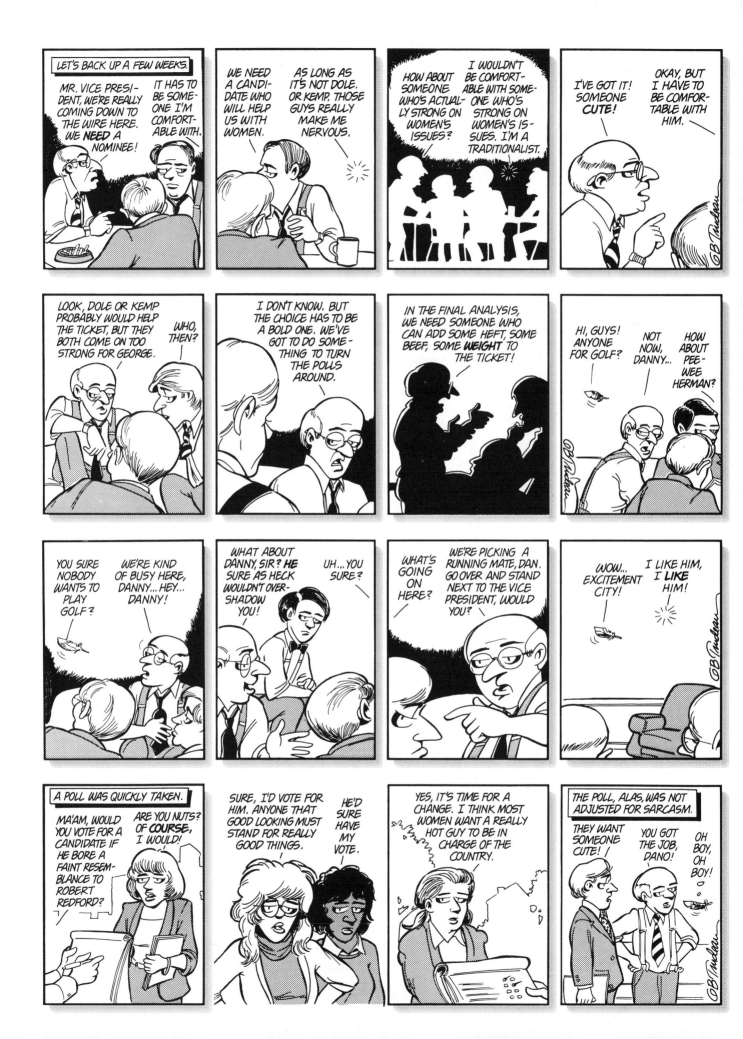

...AND WE'RE LOOKING AT A DRY, SUNNY, PERFECT 78° DAY!

SURE, WE ARE.

REALLY, IT'S NOT A TRICK.

IT BETTER NOT BE!

...AND IN DES MOINES TODAY, THE REVEREND JESSE JACKSON MADE THREE MORE APPEARANCES ON BEHALF OF THE DUKAKIS TICKET.

ROLAND HEDLEY, RECENTLY RETURNED TO ACTIVE DUTY, HAS DETAILS.

ONCE AGAIN, JESSE JACKSON HAS CONFOUNDED EXPECTATIONS, THIS TIME BY CAMPAIGNING VIGOROUSLY FOR A CANDIDATE WHO IS NOT JESSE JACKSON.

WHAT'S IN IT FOR THE FORMER PRESIDENTIAL HOPEFUL? WHAT EXACTLY DID JACKSON GET FROM THE DUKAKIS FORCES IN ATLANTA?

SOURCES WHO WERE PRESENT AT THE TIME HAVE NOW REVEALED TO ABC NEWS WHAT WAS AT THE CORE OF THE JACKSON DEAL...

"YES, FABULOUS PRIZES!"

...AND A GLAMOROUS, NEW DINETTE SET, CHOSEN ESPECIALLY FOR YOU!

JESSE JACKSON! COME ON DOWN AND SIT AT THE BIG TABLE!

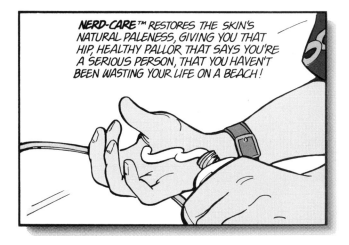

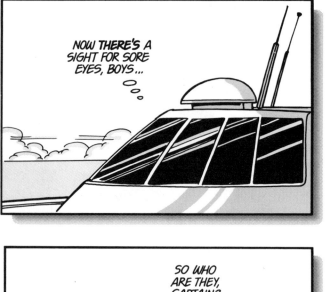

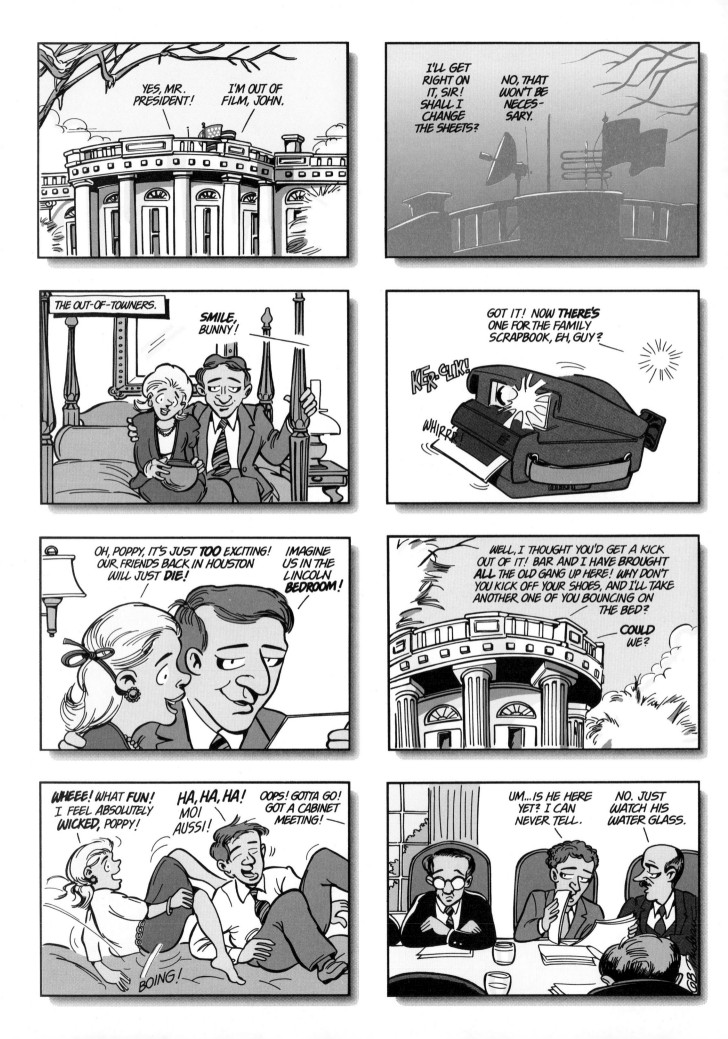

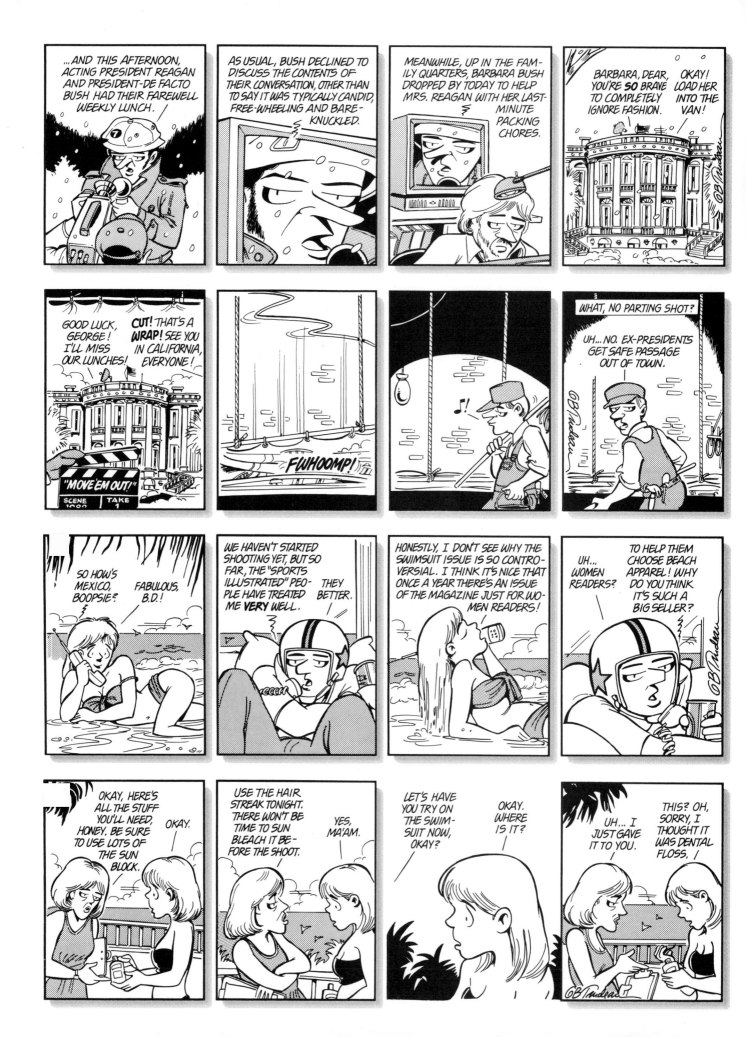

HEIDIS 03246 ANNHB

PART THREE
BRIGHT STARS, BROAD STROKES

"They came, they saw, they did a little shopping."
— Graffiti on the Berlin Wall
shortly after it was opened

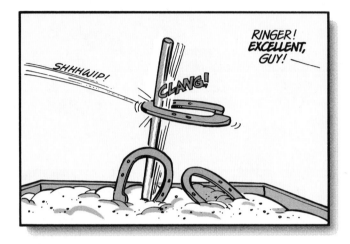

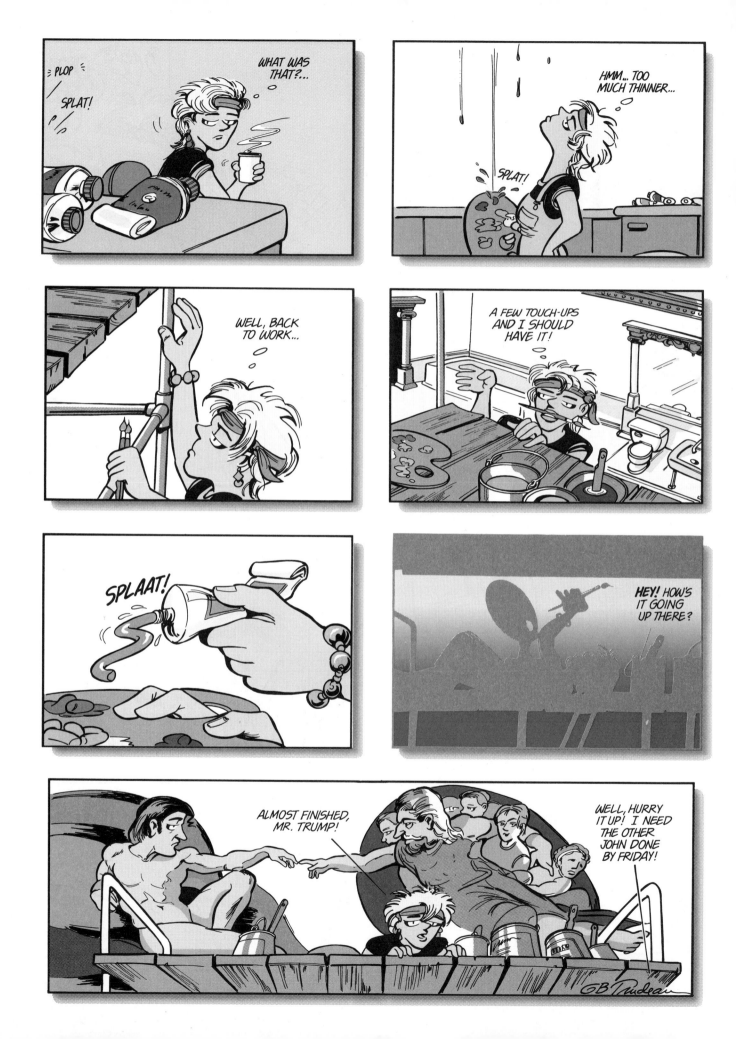

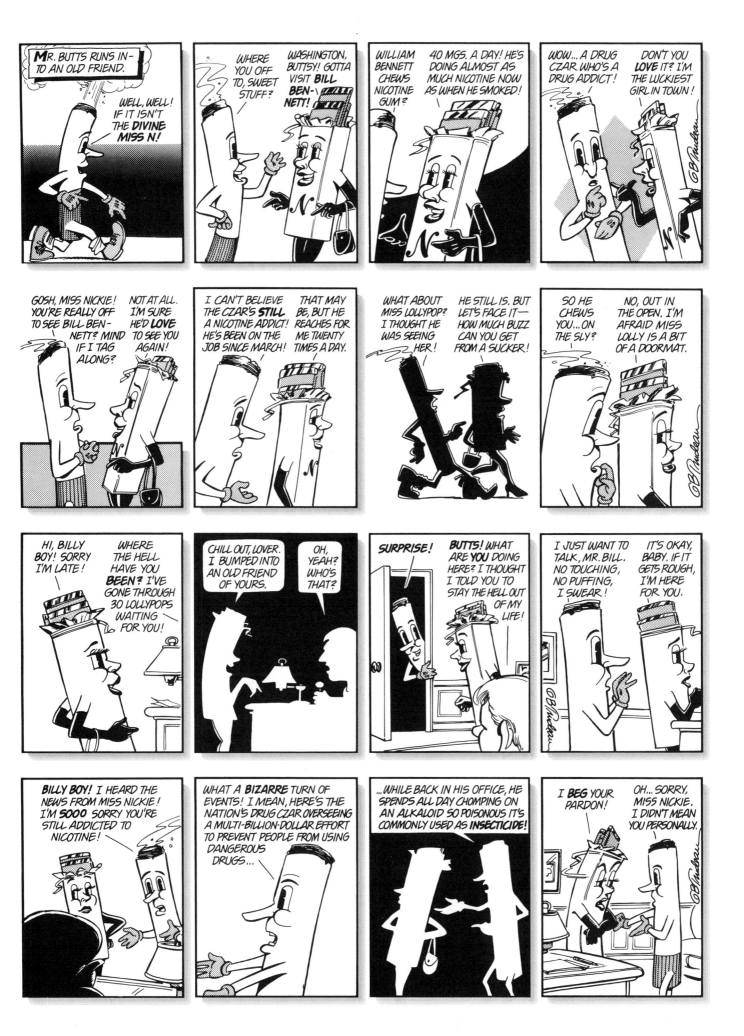